A Note to Parents

DK READERS is a compelling program for beginning readers, designed in conjunction with leading literacy experts, including Dr. Linda Gambrell, Director of the School of Education at Clemson University. Dr. Gambrell has served on the Board of Directors of the International Reading Association and as President of the National Reading Conference.

Beautiful illustrations and superb full-color photographs combine with engaging, easy-to-read stories to offer a fresh approach to each subject in the series. Each DK READER is guaranteed to capture a child's interest while developing his or her reading skills, general knowledge, and love of reading.

The five levels of DK READERS are aimed at different reading abilities, enabling you to choose the books that are exactly right for your child:

Pre-level 1: Learning to read
Level 1: Beginning to read
Level 2: Beginning to read alone
Level 3: Reading alone
Level 4: Proficient readers

The "normal" age at which a child begins to read can be anywhere from three to eight years old, so these levels are only a general guideline.

No matter which level you select, you can be sure that you are helping your child learn to read, then read to learn!

LONDON, NEW YORK, MUNICH,
MELBOURNE, and DELHI

Project Editor Naia Bray-Moffatt
Art Editor Ann Cannings
Senior Art Editor Clare Shedden
Managing Editor Bridget Gibbs
Senior DTP Designer Bridget Roseberry
U.S. Editor Regina Kahney
Production Shivani Pandey
Picture Researcher Angela Anderson
Jacket Designer Karen Burgess
Indexer Lynn Bresler
Illustrator John James

Reading Consultant
Linda Gambrell, Ph.D.

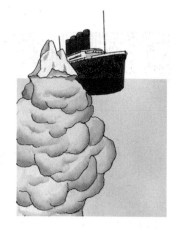

First American Edition, 2001
04 05 10 9 8 7 6 5 4 3 2
Published in the United States by DK Publishing, Inc.
375 Hudson Street, New York, New York 10014

Published in Great Britain by Dorling Kindersley Limited

Library of Congress Cataloging-in-Publication Data
Jenner, Caryn.
Titanic: a survivor's tale / by Caryn Jenner. -- 1st American ed.
p. cm. -- (Dorling Kindersley readers)
Summary: Will and Lucy sail on the Titanic and are separated
from their father when the ship hits an iceberg and begins to sink.
ISBN 0-7894-7373-9 (pbk) ISBN 0-7894-7374-7 (hc)
1. Titanic (Steamship)--Juvenile Fiction. [1. Titanic (Steamship)
--Fiction. 2. Shipwrecks--Fiction. 3. Survival--Fiction. 4. Ocean
Liners--Fiction.]
I. Title. II. Series.
PZ7.J428 Ti 2001
[Fic]--dc21   00-055520

Color reproduction by Colourscan, Singapore
Printed and bound in China by L. Rex Printing Co., Ltd.

The publisher would like to thank the following for their kind
permission to reproduce their images:
Key: t=top, a=above, b=below, l=left, r=right, c=center
Corbis UK Ltd: 2cl, 15t, 18t, 25t.
Mary Evans Picture Library: 4b.
All other images © Dorling Kindersley
For further information see: www.dkimages.com

Discover more at
www.dk.com

 READERS

Survivors
The Night the Titanic sank

Written by Caryn Jenner

DK Publishing, Inc.

What an adventure!
Will Tate looked out to sea
and grinned.
Will and his family were sailing
to America on the *Titanic*.
"The *Titanic* is the biggest ship
in the world,"
he told his little sister, Lucy.
"I know," said Lucy.
"I wish we could go upstairs.
I've heard it's like a palace!"

The passengers
Rich passengers sailed
in the ship's first-class
section. Poorer passengers
stayed in the third-class
section below.

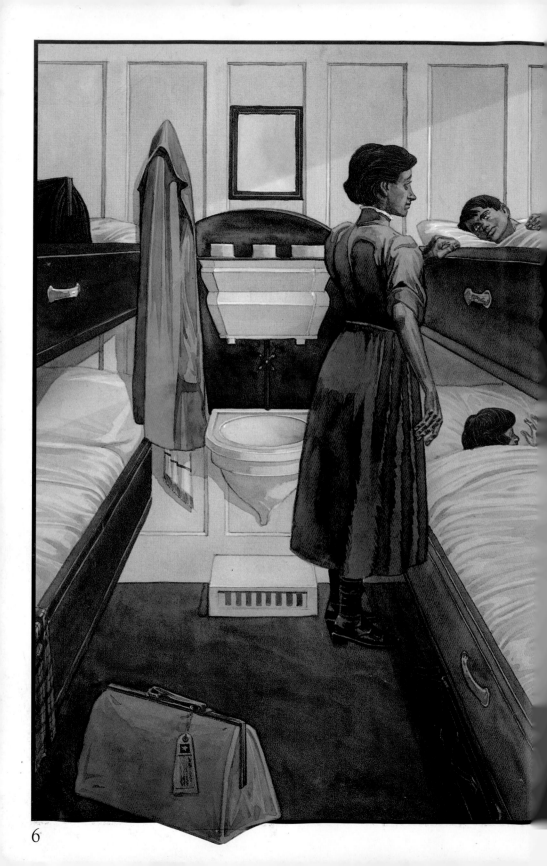

That night, Will lay in his bunk.

He listened to the hum

of the ship's engines.

"Soon we'll have

a new life in America!"

Mother whispered in the darkness.

Will smiled sleepily.

Suddenly, Will felt a hard THUMP

and then a scrape

against the side of the ship.

He nearly fell out of the bunk.

Maiden voyage
The *Titanic* took its first – and only – voyage
in 1912. It was built to a special design that
was supposed to make sinking impossible.

Will and his father
left their cabin
to see what had happened.
On the third-class deck,
they saw passengers
playing soccer with chunks of ice.
No one seemed worried.
Will kicked a chunk of ice.
"Goal!" cheered Father.
Then a ship's steward
interrupted the game.
"The ship has hit
an iceberg," he said.
"There is no danger,
but everyone should
wear a life jacket."

Hitting the iceberg

When the *Titanic* hit the iceberg, water began to flood into the hull at the bottom of the ship.

Will and Father
hurried back to their cabin.

"What is this for?" Lucy asked as she put on her life jacket.

"It will help you to float
in the water," Will told Lucy.
"Just in case."
Will watched as a bright light
shot up into the starry night sky.
It burst with a loud BANG
like a firework.
"That's an emergency flare,"
said Father.
"And there's a lifeboat.
The ship must be in trouble!"

"The lifeboats are on the top deck,"
said Father.

"Hurry!" called Mother.

The Tates ran through the ship.

It was like a big maze.

Water gushed into the hallways.

The floor slanted
and Will couldn't walk straight.

With one hand,
he gripped
a wooden railing.

With the other hand,
he pulled Lucy
up the grand staircase.
At last, they reached the top deck.

"The ship is sinking!"
cried a frightened passenger.
"But the *Titanic* is unsinkable,"
someone said calmly.
The Tates hurried
toward the lifeboats.
They weren't taking chances.

"Women and children
in the lifeboats first,"
called a ship's officer.
"I won't leave without you, Tom,"
said Mother.
"Go on, Jean," said Father.
"Take care of the children."
Mother kissed him
and climbed into
the lifeboat with Lucy.
Now it was Will's turn.

"Get in the lifeboat, Will!"
called Mother.
"Come on!" Lucy echoed.
Will didn't know what to do.
Finally, he shook his head.
"I'm staying on the ship
with Father," he said.
"Will, you must go
with your mother and
sister," said Father.
But it was too late.
Will and his father
watched as
the ship's officer
lowered the lifeboat
into the sea.

Lifeboats
The 20 lifeboats on board were not enough for all the passengers and crew.

Soon there were only a few lifeboats left. The frightened crowd pushed and shoved to climb into the boats. Will felt Father's hand on his shoulder. Suddenly, Father pushed him through the crowd and into a lifeboat.

The boat swayed
as a ship's officer
lowered it into the sea.
Will looked up
at the *Titanic*.
Father was waving
to him from the deck.

As Will helped to row the lifeboat
away from the *Titanic*,
he watched the great ship sink.
It tipped forward with a crash!

Sinking

The front of the *Titanic*
sank first. Nearly three
hours after it hit the
iceberg, the *Titanic* sank
completely under the water.

People clung to the railings.
Others jumped from the decks.
"I've got to save my father!"
called Will.
He wanted to row back
to the sinking ship.
But the other people in the
lifeboat stopped him.
"It's too dangerous," they cried.

Finally, the *Titanic* disappeared
under the water.
Somehow, Will felt sure
his father would be safe.
Some other lifeboats drifted nearby.
Using a rope,
they linked up with Will's boat.

Suddenly, he heard a familiar voice.
"Will, is that you?"
Mother was helping to row
one of the other boats!
Carefully, Will climbed into her boat
and huddled next to Lucy.

Lucy shivered.

Will put his arm around her
to keep her warm.

"Where's Father?" she asked.

"I don't know,
but I'm sure he's fine," said Will.

The cold air made his breath
look like foggy puffs.

The lifeboats drifted for a long time.

At last, Will saw a light

in the distance.

It was a rescue ship!

Everyone cheered.

It was morning by the time
the rescue ship arrived.
Will and his mother
climbed up the rope ladder.
They held on tight as the ladder
swung in the breeze.
Lucy was too little
to climb up the rope ladder.
The rescue ship's crew
pulled her aboard in a mail sack.
They were all cold, tired,
and hungry.
But finding Father
was the most important thing.

"Look! There he is!"
Will cried out at last.
He pointed to a lifeboat
that was being towed toward
the rescue ship.
"Father! Father!" called Lucy.

Father stumbled on board.
He was so cold, his lips were blue.
"I jumped from the *Titanic*
and climbed into the last lifeboat,"
he gasped.
He fell into Mother's arms.
"I'm so glad to see all of you."

Three days later,
the rescue ship
arrived in America.
Will stood on the deck
with his family as the ship docked
in New York Harbor.

"So many people
didn't survive
the shipwreck,"
said Father sadly.
"We're very lucky,"
said Mother.
Will and Lucy agreed.

There were 2,206 people
on board the *Titanic* but
only 705 survived.
The *Titanic* disaster soon
led to better safety at sea.

Modern safety at sea

Ships now carry enough lifeboats for everyone on board.

Modern technology makes it easier for ships to contact each other and to find exact locations.

The International Ice Patrol tracks icebergs from the air. With this information, ships can change course to avoid icebergs.

The *Titanic* is found! In 1985, explorers found the wreck of the *Titanic* in the Atlantic Ocean.

Other explorers use special submarines and robots to take pictures and bring back objects from the shipwreck.